RESPONSIVE CSS3 SCROLLING EFFECTS

STEP BY STEP TRAINING

Learn by doing step by step exercises.
Includes downloadable class files that work on Mac & PC.

EDITION 1.3

Published by:
Noble Desktop LLC
594 Broadway, Suite 1202
New York, NY 10012
www.nobledesktop.com

Copyright © 2013–2017 Noble Desktop LLC
Publish Date: 06-13-2017

All rights reserved. No part of this book may be reproduced or transmitted in any form by any means, electronic, mechanical, photocopy, recording, or otherwise without express written permission from the publisher. For information on reprint rights, please contact **educator-in-chief@nobledesktop.com**

The publisher makes no representations or warranties with respect to the accuracy or completeness of the contents of this work, and specifically disclaims any warranties. Noble Desktop shall not have any liability to any person or entity with respect to any loss or damage caused or alleged to be caused directly or indirectly by the instructions contained in this book or by the computer software and hardware products described in it. Further, readers should be aware that software updates can make some of the instructions obsolete, and that websites listed in this work may have changed or disappeared since publication.

Adobe, the Adobe Logo, Creative Cloud, InDesign, Illustrator, Photoshop, and Dreamweaver are trademarks of Adobe Systems Incorporated.

Apple and macOS are trademarks of Apple Inc. registered in the U.S. and other countries. Microsoft and Windows are either registered trademarks or trademarks of Microsoft Corporation in the U.S. and other countries. All other trademarks are the property of their respective owners.

Table of Contents

SETUP & INTRODUCTION

Downloading the Class Files 5

INFO & EXERCISES

SECTION 1

Exercise 1A: Styling the Photos & Text 7

Exercise 1B: Creating an Animated CSS Transition for a YouTube Video 21

Exercise 1C: Animating the Panorama & Making the Layout Responsive 27

REFERENCE MATERIAL

Noble's Other Workbooks 41

Downloading the Class Files

Thank You for Purchasing a Noble Desktop Course Workbook!
These instructions tell you how to install the class files you'll need to go through the exercises in this workbook.

Downloading & Installing Class Files

1. Navigate to the **Desktop.**

2. Create a **new folder** called **Class Files** (this is where you'll put the files after they have been downloaded).

3. Go to nobledesktop.com/download

4. Enter the code **rse-1706-13**

5. If you haven't already, click **Start Download.**

6. After the **.zip** file has finished downloading, be sure to unzip the file if it hasn't been done for you. You should end up with a **Responsive CSS3 Scrolling Effects** folder.

7. Drag the downloaded folder into the **Class Files** folder you just made. These are the files you will use while going through the workbook.

8. If you still have the downloaded .zip file, you can delete that. That's it! Enjoy.

Styling the Photos & Text

1A

Exercise Preview

Exercise Overview

Throughout the exercises in this book, you will code an image-rich webpage and learn how to take advantage of the awesome native CSS capabilities of modern browsers. You'll build an elegant, responsive design where all content—including images and videos—resizes in accordance with browser size. You will also explore techniques for using CSS animated transitions that zoom, pan, and scroll. Along the way, you'll use media queries to fine tune the content so it displays beautifully in any size browser, from a mobile device to a wide-screen display.

In this exercise you'll get started by styling sections that have photo backgrounds which remain fixed on-screen while their text scrolls over top.

Getting Started

Before we get coding, let's look at a finished version of the webpage we're about to create and check out all of its great new CSS features.

1. Open a web browser. To see all the effects built into this page you'll need to use Chrome, Safari, Firefox, or Internet Explorer 10+. Internet Explorer 9 and older do not support all the features.

2. To open a file, hit **Command–O** (Mac) or **Control–O** (Windows).

3. Navigate into **Desktop > Class Files > Responsive CSS3 Scrolling Effects > Hawaii Done** and double-click on **index.html** to open it.

   We want to do a quick survey of all the highlights of the finished webpage.

4. First, make sure your browser window is as large as possible so you're looking at the desktop design.

1A Styling the Photos & Text

5. Scroll through the site, and take note of the following:

   - The full-size background images don't scroll along with the page, as is customary, but have a special static or "sticky" behavior.

   - The Mt. Haleakala image displays as a moving panorama.

   - Web fonts are fully integrated and the title fonts have a subtle shadow.

   - The YouTube video zooms to full-size when you mouse over it.

   - Most exciting of all, when you resize the browser window, note the responsive behavior of all the text and image elements. Much of the coding we'll be doing will focus on ensuring that the page looks great in any size browser.

   These are the CSS features you'll soon see how to implement!

6. Let's get to work! Launch your preferred code editor (such as **Sublime Text, Atom, Dreamweaver,** etc.).

7. Open the following file: **Desktop > Class Files > Responsive CSS3 Scrolling Effects > Hawaii > index.html** (Be sure to go into the **Hawaii** folder, not one of the **Done** folders.)

   If you're using a code editor that allows you to open an entire project folder, such as **Sublime Text,** we suggest you open the **Hawaii** folder.

8. This file **(index.html)** is contains the text for the Hawaii webpage and some of the basic layout. On line 8 note the **viewport meta** tag.

   ```
   <meta name="viewport" content="width=device-width, initial-scale=1">
   ```

   We added this code to save you some work, but it's important to know that this tag is required for responsive pages to display properly on mobile devices.

9. Let's check this page out in a web browser so we can see what work we need to do. Open a web browser and hit **Command–O** (Mac) or **Control–O** (Windows).

10. Navigate to **Responsive CSS3 Scrolling Effects > Hawaii** and **double–click** on **index.html** to open it.

11. Resize the window, making it narrower and wider. Notice how the main text column has a max-width of 1000 pixels. This prevents the lines from getting too long to comfortably read, but allows for it to get narrower on small screens. When made narrower, the text already flows responsively because elements like the callout (pull quote) have a percentage-based width.

    At this point the page is devoid of images, but there are text-based placeholders where we are going to make the photo panorama and the photo stack.

Styling the Photos & Text

Coding the Image Styles

Because we want the images to do various things (such as animate or stay fixed as we scroll) we'll create **div** tags for them instead of using **img** tags.

1. Switch back to **index.html** in your code editor.

2. Around line 17 add the following bold code:

   ```
   <div class="page-layout">
      <div class="feature-wrap">

      </div>
      <div class="main-wrap">
   ```

   By default, divs are 100% of the width of their parent element. We do want this div to be full-width, so that's all set, but we also want the div to have a 2-pixel border at the top. We will have to add this in the CSS file.

3. Save **index.html**.

4. Open the following file: **Hawaii > css > style.css**

5. Take a brief look at the **style.css** file and notice that some basic CSS styles have already been defined to save you some work.

6. Let's create a **feature-wrap** rule to create 2-pixel borders at the top and bottom of the div. Find the **.main-wrap** rule (around line 22) and add the following bold code underneath it:

   ```
   .main-wrap {
      max-width: 1000px;
      margin: 45px auto;
      padding: 0 15px;
      font-family: 'Vollkorn', Georgia, serif;
   }
   .feature-wrap {
      border-top: 2px solid #181818;
      border-bottom: 2px solid #181818;
   }
   ```

7. Save **style.css**.

8. Preview **index.html** in a web browser. Look very carefully for the dark border at the very top of the page. This will look much better once we get a picture inside.

   NOTE: We recommend leaving the page open in the browser while you work so you can simply reload it to see each change.

9. Switch to **index.html** in your code editor.

1A Styling the Photos & Text

10. Let's take a moment to think about how we'll code the page. We will have four **feature-wrap** divs, each containing photo highlights and text descriptions. Although the photos will share some of the same styles, each feature photo will have slight variations on the theme. It will be useful to lay out each separate photo feature as its own self-contained module—or div— that sits inside the feature-wrap div. Let's start by adding the div we'll use for the lead photo and header information.

11. Around line 18, inside the **feature-wrap** div, add a new div for photo feature headings, like so:

    ```
    <div class="feature-wrap">
        <div class="photo lead">

        </div>
    </div>
    ```

    Note that we'll use the **photo** class to share styles with all feature photos but the second class **(lead)** will be used to vary the style from feature to feature.

12. Next, let's add some variously sized header text that will overlay the photograph in the newly created div. Type the following bold code:

    ```
    <div class="photo lead">
        <h3>Dan Rodney | May 2</h3>
        <h1>The Islands of Hawaii</h1>
        <h2>Diverse and Majestic</h2>
    </div>
    ```

13. Save the file.

14. Switch to **style.css**.

15. Scroll down to the very bottom of the file and add the following style:

    ```
    .feature-wrap .lead {
        padding: 10% 0 30% 0;
    }
    ```

    Because we want this site to be a really responsive webpage, the padding values will often be **percentages** rather than absolute values.

    NOTE: The order of four padding values goes clockwise starting at the top, or if you prefer a mnemonic: **Top, Right, Bottom, Left** = TRBL (Trouble).

16. Save **style.css.**

17. Reload **index.html** in your web browser. Notice the large headings, and try resizing the browser window in various ways to see how the 10% top padding and 30% bottom padding behave responsively to the changing window size.

18. Return to **style.css** in your code editor.

Styling the Photos & Text

19. Add a background image to the **lead** style by adding the bold code as follows:

    ```
    .feature-wrap .lead {
       padding: 10% 0 30% 0;
       background-image: url(../img/lead.jpg);
    }
    ```

20. Save the file and reload the browser. The background image is there, but the photo is very large and you may only be able to see a portion of the top-left corner. Resize the page to see that the background image doesn't change size, it's just being cropped.

    We want to see the whole **lead** background image and also have it resize responsively when we change the page size. In fact, we want all of our images to behave in this manner, so we should create a rule for the **photo** class.

21. Return to **style.css** and add the following bold code directly above the **.feature-wrap .lead** rule:

    ```
    .feature-wrap .photo {
       background-repeat: no-repeat;
       background-position: center;
       background-size: cover;
    }
    ```

22. Here's how the new style breaks down:

    - **background-repeat: no-repeat** ensures that the image doesn't repeat (or tile) in an unsightly way.

    - **background-position: center** will center align the image both horizontally and vertically.

    - **background-size: cover** is a great new feature of CSS3 that tells the image to always scale up or down to fill the area, no matter the window size. This way we'll always have as much of the photo showing as possible!

23. Save the file and reload the browser to see the changes.

    - To see how the **background-size: cover** feature works, resize the page to different proportions.

    - Scroll up and down on the page. Currently the background image scrolls with the page, but we want to make it stay static as we scroll.

24. Return to **style.css** in your code editor.

1A Styling the Photos & Text

25. Add the following bold code:

    ```
    .feature-wrap .photo {
       background-repeat: no-repeat;
       background-position: center;
       background-size: cover;
       background-attachment: fixed;
    }
    ```

26. Save the file and reload the browser. Try scrolling now, and see the new, fancier "static" behavior of the background image! You may notice that the cover setting is no longer working the same way. In wide windows it still works as expected, but when the window is narrower the photo becomes cropped instead of scaling to fit.

    NOTE: **background-attachment** works well on desktops, but not on mobile devices. It's not supported in Android Browser. iOS has a known conflict between **background-attachment: fixed** and **background-size: cover** that causes the image to be scaled to cover the full length of the webpage (so it gets really stretched out). In a later exercise we'll disable the **background-attachment: fixed** on mobile devices, so it will only work on desktops.

Styling the Header Text

Our headings incorporate custom fonts from Google Fonts. We've already loaded the fonts to save you some work. If you've never used Google Fonts on your own before, you can find out more at fonts.google.com

1. Return to **style.css** in your code editor.

2. Let's work on styling the header text. Around line 28, find the **.feature-wrap** style and add the following new style below it:

   ```
   .lead h1 {
      font-family: 'Rye', cursive;
      font-weight: 400;
      font-size: 3.6em;
      line-height: 1em;
      text-transform: uppercase;
   }
   ```

3. Save **style.css** and reload the browser to see your changes. What a snazzy typeface.

4. Return to **style.css** in your code editor.

Styling the Photos & Text

5. The heading looks a bit too close to the left-hand margin. Add the following code to add responsive margins to the top, right, and left of the **h1** heading:

   ```
   .lead h1 {
       font-family: 'Rye', cursive;
       font-weight: 400;
       font-size: 3.6em;
       line-height: 1em;
       text-transform: uppercase;
       margin: 1% 10% 0 10%;
   }
   ```

6. Save the file and reload the browser. Great, the spacing around the heading is much more balanced! Let's fix up the other headings to look just as good.

7. Return to **style.css** in your code editor.

8. Add the following two new styles beneath the **.lead h1** style (which starts around line 32):

   ```
   .lead h2 {
       font-family: 'Quicksand', sans-serif;
       font-size: 1.6em;
       line-height: 1em;
       text-transform: uppercase;
       margin: 1% 10% 0 10%;
   }
   .lead h3 {
       font-family: 'Quicksand', sans-serif;
       font-weight: 400;
       font-size: 1.05em;
       text-transform: uppercase;
       margin: 0 10%;
   }
   ```

   NOTE: The **h3** style has only two margins defined. The **first value** applies to the **top** and **bottom** margins, and the **second value** applies to the **left** and **right** margins. It's a quicker way of writing **margin: 0 10% 0 10%** and it looks cleaner too!

9. Save the file and reload the browser.

   Check out those new text styles. They're all aligned nicely. Again, all of the margins are percentage-based, so if you resize the window to different sizes and proportions, the spacing and margins will change in subtle ways, ensuring that the site looks beautiful in any browser. Our header section is looking good for now. Let's move on to coding and styling the photo panorama.

1A Styling the Photos & Text

Styling the Photo Panorama

1. The photo panorama will be another full-width **feature-wrap** section. Switch to **index.html** in your code editor.

2. Scroll down until you find the words **photo panorama** (around line 48).

3. Delete the words **photo panorama.**

4. In the empty space, type the following:

   ```
   <div class="feature-wrap">
      <div class="photo panorama">

      </div>
   </div>
   ```

5. Save the file.

6. Switch to **style.css.**

7. Add the following style at the very bottom of the file:

   ```
   .feature-wrap .panorama {
      padding: 10% 0;
      background-image: url(../img/panorama.jpg);
   }
   ```

   Keep in mind that the **.panorama** is also inheriting all the features of the **.photo** style that we defined earlier (like background-size), so we only have to specify the things that will be different about the panorama section.

8. Save the file and preview **index.html** in the browser.

   Scroll down to see that the panorama photo is looking good! Notice it has inherited the **cover** property and the special static scrolling behavior from the **.photo** style.

9. Later on we will add a panoramic scrolling animation, but we're not going to worry about that yet. First let's work on the text that will overlay the panorama. Switch to **index.html** in your code editor.

10. Create a new div by typing the following around line 50:

    ```
    <div class="photo panorama">
       <div class="text">

       </div>
    </div>
    ```

Styling the Photos & Text

11. This div will contain the panorama text. Type the following:

    ```
    <div class="text">
       Mt. Haleakala's southern face is vastly different from the north.
    </div>
    ```

12. Save the file.

13. Switch to **style.css.**

14. Create a new style at the very bottom of the document:

    ```
    .feature-wrap .text {
       font-family: 'Rye', sans-serif;
       font-size: 3em;
       line-height: 1.1em;
       color: #f1f1f1;
       text-align: center;
       margin: 0 25%;
       text-shadow: 0 0 4px rgba(0,0,0, 0.5);
    }
    ```

    The text styling exists inside the **.feature-wrap** module because we only want this style to be used in the featured photograph areas.

15. The **text-shadow** property is a great new feature of CSS3. It will make our text easier to read as it floats over the images. Here is how that line of code breaks down:

    - **text-shadow: 0 0** These two numbers are the x-offset and y-offset (setting them both to zero will position the shadow directly behind the text).

    - **4px** This number controls the blur size of the shadow. A larger number will create a larger shadow.

    - **rgba(0,0,0, 0.5)** The letters stand for red, green, blue, alpha (alpha means transparency). Setting all the RGB values to zero (as we just did) makes the shadow color black. The alpha works differently, on a scale from 0.0 to 1.0, where 0.0 is transparent and 1.0 is opaque. Because we set the value to **0.5,** the text shadow will be 50% transparent.

16. Save the file and reload the browser.

    Check out the new style on the panorama text! The text shadow makes the blurb easier to read in light areas, and the percentage-based responsive margins keep the text perfectly centered when you resize the browser window.

    The panorama section is looking good for now, so let's move on to coding another one of the site's photo highlights.

1A Styling the Photos & Text

Styling the Photo Stack

The next photo section we need to code is a **photo stack:** three large photos that will each occupy the entire screen as the viewer scrolls down the page.

1. Switch to **index.html** in your code editor.

2. Scroll down until you see the words **photo stack** around line 76.

3. Delete the words **photo stack**.

4. In the empty space, type the following:

```
<div class="feature-wrap">
   <div class="photo stack">
      <div class="text">
         Hawaiian Luau: Good food & hula dancers!
      </div>
   </div>
</div>
```

5. Great! Our photo stack has three pictures, though. Because we want the second and third sections of the photo stack to behave like the one we just created, copy everything you just typed.

6. Paste the code **two times** below. You should end up with a total of **three** chunks of identical code.

Styling the Photos & Text

7. Add the captions as shown below in bold:

```
<div class="feature-wrap">
   <div class="photo stack">
      <div class="text">
         Hawaiian Luau: Good food & hula dancers!
      </div>
   </div>
</div>
<div class="feature-wrap">
   <div class="photo stack">
      <div class="text">
         You're going to need a boat to get here!
      </div>
   </div>
</div>
<div class="feature-wrap">
   <div class="photo stack">
      <div class="text">
         Watch the sun rise from above. You're standing outside looking down at the clouds!
      </div>
   </div>
</div>
```

8. Save the file and reload the browser. Scroll down to see the three blocks of text we just typed against the white background, with the dark div borders above and below. They're very close together, so let's add some padding.

9. Switch to **style.css** in your code editor.

10. Add a new style for the photo stack around line 102, directly above the **.feature-wrap .text** style. Type the following:

```
.feature-wrap .stack {
   padding: 55% 0;
}
```

11. Save the file and reload the browser. Now each caption has plenty of space around it—each photo stack div is at least 110% of the browser window's height because there is 55% padding on the top and 55% padding on the bottom. This is exactly what we want in order to make each photo take up the entire screen as the viewer scrolls down the page.

12. We have spots for three different stack photos, but we don't yet have a way to style them uniquely. Let's fix that. Switch to **index.html** in your code editor.

1A Styling the Photos & Text

13. Make the changes shown below to differentiate each of the photo stack divs:

    ```
    <div class="feature-wrap">
       <div class="photo stack stack-one">
          <div class="text">
             Hawaiian Luau: Good food & hula dancers!
          </div>
       </div>
    </div>
    <div class="feature-wrap">
       <div class="photo stack stack-two">
          <div class="text">
             You're going to need a boat to get here!
          </div>
       </div>
    </div>
    <div class="feature-wrap">
       <div class="photo stack stack-three">
          <div class="text">
             Watch the sunrise from above the clouds. You're standing outside looking down at the clouds!
          </div>
       </div>
    </div>
    ```

14. Save the file.

15. Switch to **style.css.**

16. Below the **.feature-wrap .stack** style (which starts around line 102) type the following style:

    ```
    .feature-wrap .stack-one {
       background-image: url(../img/luau.jpg);
    }
    ```

17. Copy what you just typed.

18. Paste it **twice** below (for a total of **three** chunks of identical code) as follows:

    ```
    .feature-wrap .stack-one {
       background-image: url(../img/luau.jpg);
    }
    .feature-wrap .stack-one {
       background-image: url(../img/luau.jpg);
    }
    .feature-wrap .stack-one {
       background-image: url(../img/luau.jpg);
    }
    ```

Styling the Photos & Text

19. Change the photo filenames and the numbers of the stacks as shown below:

    ```
    .feature-wrap .stack-one {
       background-image: url(../img/luau.jpg);
    }
    .feature-wrap .stack-two {
       background-image: url(../img/coast.jpg);
    }
    .feature-wrap .stack-three {
       background-image: url(../img/clouds.jpg);
    }
    ```

20. Save the file and reload the browser.

    The photo stack should be looking very good. The images are static and the text scrolls as we move down the page.

    Maybe it's a bit boring to keep all the text centered, though. Let's change up the text alignment by creating classes that will let us align some of the text blurbs to the left and align others to the right.

21. Switch to **index.html** in your code editor.

22. Find the following code and make the changes in bold:

    ```
    <div class="feature-wrap">
       <div class="photo stack stack-one">
          <div class="text left">
             Hawaiian Luau: Good food & hula dancers!
          </div>
       </div>
    </div>
    <div class="feature-wrap">
       <div class="photo stack stack-two">
          <div class="text right">
             You're going to need a boat to get here!
          </div>
       </div>
    </div>
    <div class="feature-wrap">
       <div class="photo stack stack-three">
          <div class="text left">
             Watch the sun rise from above the clouds. You're standing outside looking down at the clouds!
          </div>
       </div>
    </div>
    ```

23. Save the file.

24. Switch to **style.css.**

1A Styling the Photos & Text

25. Scroll to the bottom of the file and add the following rule to make sure that the photo stack text is a bit narrower, only 35% of the width of the parent div:

    ```
    .feature-wrap .stack .text {
       width: 35%;
    }
    ```

26. Below that, add a rule for left aligned text with a small left-hand margin:

    ```
    .feature-wrap .stack .text.left {
       text-align: left;
       margin: 0 0 0 10%;
    }
    ```

27. Almost done styling this text! Add the right aligned style as follows:

    ```
    .feature-wrap .stack .text.left {
       text-align: left;
       margin: 0 0 0 10%;
    }
    .feature-wrap .stack .text.right {
       text-align: right;
       margin: 0 0 0 50%;
    }
    ```

28. Save the file and reload the browser. Scroll down to check out the improvements to the photo stack! The text looks much more sophisticated with the latest changes.

    We've done the basic styling on the three major **feature-wrap** sections of the site. It's really coming along!

Creating an Animated CSS Transition for a YouTube Video — 1B

Exercise Preview

Hawaii's tallest mountain, Mauna Kea, stands at 13,796 feet but is taller than Mount Everest if followed to the base of the mountain, which, lying at the floor of the Pacific Ocean, rises about 33,500 feet.

The eight main islands, Hawai'i, Maui, O'ahu, Kaho'olawe, Lana'i, Moloka'i, Kaua'i and Ni'ihau are accompanied by many others. Ka'ala is a small island near Ni'ihau that is often overlooked. The Northwest Hawaiian Islands are a series of nine small, older masses northwest of Kaua'i that extend from Nihoa to Kure that are remnants of once much larger volcanic mountains. There are also more than 100 small rocks and islets, such as Molokini, that are either volcanic, marine sedimentary or erosional in origin, totaling 130 or so across the archipelago.

The Hawaiian islands were (and continue to be) continuously formed from volcanic activity initiated at an undersea magma source called a hotspot. As the tectonic plate beneath much of the Pacific Ocean moves to the northwest, the hot spot remains stationary, slowly creating new volcanoes. Due to the hotspot's location, the only active volcanoes are located around the

Exercise Overview

In this exercise you'll add a YouTube video that enlarges when you mouse over it. You'll use a CSS transition so it enlarges smoothly, with no JavaScript required!

1. If you completed the previous exercise, **index.html** should still be open in your code editor, and you can skip the following sidebar. If you closed **index.html**, re-open it now. We recommend you finish the previous exercise (1A) before starting this one. If you haven't finished it, do the following sidebar.

   > **If You Did Not Do the Previous Exercise (1A)**
   >
   > 1. Close any files you may have open.
   > 2. On the **Desktop**, go to **Class Files > Responsive CSS3 Scrolling Effects.**
   > 3. Delete the **Hawaii** folder if it exists.
   > 4. Duplicate the **Hawaii Photos & Text Done** folder.
   > 5. Rename it to **Hawaii** and if possible, open it in your code editor.

1B Creating an Animated CSS Transition for a YouTube Video

Positioning & Sizing the YouTube Video

1. In **index.html,** around line 107 add the following bold code to create a home for the YouTube video:

   ```
   <p>
       Hawaii's tallest mountain, Mauna Kea, stands at 13,796 feet but is taller
   than Mount Everest if followed to the base of the mountain, which, lying at
   the floor of the Pacific Ocean, rises about 33,500 feet.
   </p>
   <div class="zoom">
       <div class="video-wrap">

       </div>
   </div>
   <p>
       The eight main islands, Hawai'i, Maui, O'ahu, Kaho'olawe, Lana'i, Moloka'i,
   Kaua'i and Ni'ihau are accompanied by many others.
   ```

2. Save the file.

3. Open **style.css** (in the **css** folder).

4. Scroll down to the very bottom of the file and add the following style:

   ```
   .zoom {
       float: right;
       width: 40%;
       margin: 7px 20px 15px 7px;
       padding: 5px;
       border: 1px solid #000;
   }
   ```

5. Save the file and reload the browser.

   Scroll down until you see the small, empty rectangle, the video's future home. We won't need the border and padding for the final design but it's helpful to have them here to gauge the size and positioning of the video wrapper as you work. Try changing the proportions of the browser window and see how the video div resizes automatically to occupy 40% of the browser's width.

   It's pretty easy to tell a div to resize to a certain percentage of a browser's width, like we just did. Unfortunately, it will be trickier to make the box's height resize in proportion to the browser window while maintaining the video's 16:9 aspect ratio—this is because there is no height unit that will take into account the page's width.

   The solution to getting the box to resize in height proportionally as we change the page's width is to use some percentage-based padding to hold the box open! Percentage-based padding will use the width of the box as the value of its percentage. Let's add that now.

Creating an Animated CSS Transition for a YouTube Video   1B

6. Return to **style.css** in your code editor.

7. At the very bottom of the file add the following style:

   ```
   .video-wrap {
       padding-top: 56.25%;
   }
   ```

   This means that whatever the width of the box, we want the height to be 56.25% of that width. How did we come up with that number? The aspect ratio of the video is 16:9, and 9/16 = 56.25%.

8. Save the file and reload the browser.

   While looking at the video box (towards the bottom of the page), try changing the proportions of the browser window. This is perfect! The box maintains the 16:9 aspect ratio as it resizes.

9. Return to your code editor.

10. Open **Hawaii > snippets > youtube-iframe.html** This is the standard embed code that YouTube gives you when you click on **Share**. This will allow us to embed their video into our page.

11. Select all the code in the file.

12. Copy the code.

13. Close **youtube-iframe.html.**

14. Switch to **index.html** in your code editor.

15. Paste the code you just copied into the **video-wrap** div (around line 109):

    ```
    <div class="zoom">
       <div class="video-wrap">
          <iframe width="560" height="315" src="https://www.youtube.com/embed/G0K9Ht0N_as?rel=0" frameborder="0" allowfullscreen></iframe>
       </div>
    </div>
    ```

16. Save the file and reload the browser.

    The YouTube video is appearing on the page, but it still needs some work. We need to position the video over the padding in the box, and make sure that the width and height of the video corresponds to the size of the box. Let's use absolute positioning to get it where we want it!

17. Switch to **style.css** in your code editor.

1B Creating an Animated CSS Transition for a YouTube Video

18. Towards the bottom of the file, add the following code shown in bold:

    ```
    .video-wrap {
        padding-top: 56.25%;
        position: relative;
    }
    ```

    We're going to use absolute positioning to position the iframe inside our **.video-wrap.** Therefore we need to declare a position (relative or absolute) on the nearest parent element that we wish to use as a positioning anchor. If we don't declare a position on the nearest relative parent (in this case the **.video-wrap**), the **body** tag will be used as the positioning anchor. Now the iframe inside the wrapper can use absolute positioning relative to the wrapper itself.

19. At the very bottom of the document, add a rule for the **iframe** that'll hold the video:

    ```
    .video-wrap iframe {
        position: absolute;
        top: 0;
        left: 0;
        width: 100%;
        height: 100%;
    }
    ```

    This style specifies that the **iframe** (which is a child of the **.video-wrap**) is using absolute positioning to be placed in the upper left corner of the wrapper.

20. Save the file and reload the browser.

    Looking excellent! The YouTube video should be sitting over the top of the padding. Even better, since we told it to take up 100% of the width and height of the available space, it should resize perfectly if you play around with changing the proportions and size of the browser window. Now we have a fully responsive, easily resizing video.

21. Return to **style.css** in your code editor.

22. We no longer need the **border** and **padding** on the rule for the zoom div, so **delete** those two properties. When you're done, the rule for **.zoom** should read as follows:

    ```
    .zoom {
        float: right;
        width: 40%;
        margin: 7px 20px 15px 7px;
    }
    ```

Creating an Animated CSS Transition for a YouTube Video   1B

Adding an Animated CSS Transition on Hover

1. We also want our video to actually zoom when a visitor hovers over it! Let's make that style now. Add the following code below the **zoom** rule (which starts around line 134), as shown below:

   ```
   .zoom:hover {
      width: 100%;
      margin: 15px 0;
   }
   ```

   This new class ensures that when a visitor mouses over (hovers over) the video, it will expand to be 100% of the width of the browser.

2. Save the file and reload the browser. Great! Our hover style should be working! However, it is rather jumpy as it switches from occupying 40% to 100% of the browser's width. Let's add an animation that makes this move less jerky.

3. Return to **style.css** in your code editor.

4. Let's implement another cool new CSS3 feature: the ability to animate transitions between two states. We can specify that whenever any property in our zoom class undergoes a change, that change should be animated. Add the following bold code:

   ```
   .zoom {
      float: right;
      width: 40%;
      margin: 7px 20px 15px 7px;
      transition: all 0.4s ease-in-out;
   }
   ```

   This rule says to transition **all** of the properties (in our case, that will include changes to the width and margins) over the course of **0.4** seconds. The **ease-in-out** option slows the animation at the beginning and end.

5. The **transition** property works in modern browsers, but not in some older browsers (such as the older Android Browser). We can add a **-webkit** vendor prefixed version to make it function in more browsers. Copy the line of code you just wrote and paste a copy as shown below:

   ```
   .zoom {
      float: right;
      width: 40%;
      margin: 7px 20px 15px 7px;
      transition: all 0.4s ease-in-out;
      transition: all 0.4s ease-in-out;
   }
   ```

1B Creating an Animated CSS Transition for a YouTube Video

6. Add the **-webkit** vendor prefix to the first one, as shown below in bold:

   ```
   -webkit-transition: all 0.4s ease-in-out;
   transition: all 0.4s ease-in-out;
   ```

   NOTE: The unprefixed property (the official CSS that all browsers should use) always goes after the prefixed properties. How long you include a **-webkit** vendor prefixed version of this property will depend on how long you want to support older browsers. For info about browser support refer to **caniuse.com/#feat=css-transitions**

7. Save the file and preview **index.html** in the web browser. Try hovering over the video to see its amazing CSS3-powered zoom animation! How incredible that we can make this animation just using CSS, no Flash or JavaScript required.

Animating the Panorama & Making the Layout Responsive 1C

Exercise Preview

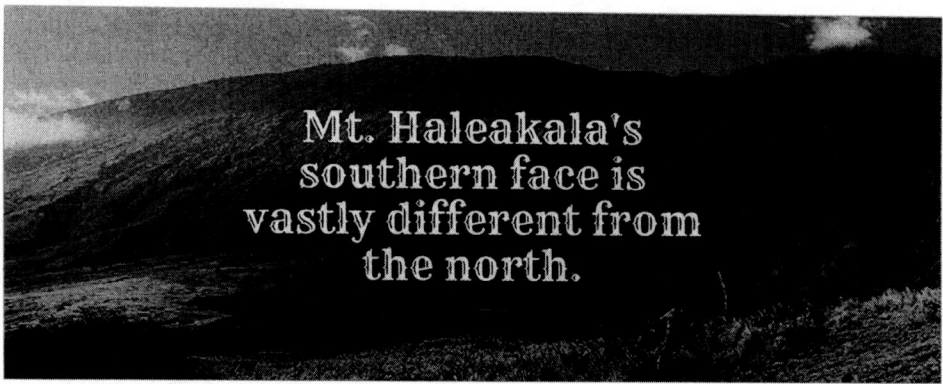

Exercise Overview

The first thing you'll do in this exercise is animate the panorama background photo, so it pans back and forth. You'll then finish up the layout by making it responsive, so it adapts to any size screen.

1. If you completed the previous exercise, **style.css** should still be open, and you can skip the following sidebar. If you closed **style.css,** re-open it now. We recommend you finish the previous exercises (1A–1B) before starting this one. If you haven't finished them, do the following sidebar.

> **If You Did Not Do the Previous Exercises (1A–1B)**
>
> 1. Close any files you may have open.
> 2. On the **Desktop,** go to **Class Files > Responsive CSS3 Scrolling Effects.**
> 3. Delete the **Hawaii** folder if it exists.
> 4. Duplicate the **Hawaii YouTube Done** folder.
> 5. Rename it to **Hawaii** and if possible, open it in your code editor.

Animating the Panorama Background

Right now we have a very wide image in the panorama segment of the page, and we can only see a small portion of the vista. We want to make the background image scroll slowly from left to right.

We can't use a transition on this element because we're not changing between two different states. Instead, we have to create a CSS animation.

1C Animating the Panorama & Making the Layout Responsive

1. Scroll down to the bottom of **style.css** and add the following code at the very end of the document:

   ```
   @keyframes moving-bg {
   
   }
   ```

2. Define the animation's starting and ending keyframes by adding this bold code:

   ```
   @keyframes moving-bg {
       0% {
           background-position: 0 0;
       }
       100% {
           background-position: 100% 0;
       }
   }
   ```

   The above positions are indicated by **x, y** coordinates. This code means that the starting position keyframe will be at **0 0** (the upper left corner of the image), and the ending position keyframe will be at the point when all of the image (**100%**) has moved to the right. The **x** position of the image will change from **0** to **100%** while the **y** position remains constant (at zero), thereby achieving the "panning" effect with our very long, narrow background image.

3. Find the **.feature-wrap .panorama** class (around line 98). Add the background animation to the class with the following bold code:

   ```
   .feature-wrap .panorama {
       padding: 10% 0;
       background-image: url(../img/panorama.jpg);
       animation: moving-bg 20s linear infinite alternate;
   }
   ```

4. A breakdown of the line of code you just wrote:

   - **moving-bg** is the name of our animation.
   - **20s** is the length of the animation, 20 seconds.
   - **linear** stands for linear easing, ensuring that the animation moves smoothly.
   - **infinite** means the animation will repeat infinitely.
   - **alternate** means that, once the animation ends, it will repeat in the alternate direction (i.e., go left to right, then right to left) for a seamless look.

5. Save the file and preview **index.html** a browser to see the photo behind the **Mt. Haleakala** text should be moving!

6. Return to your code editor.

Animating the Panorama & Making the Layout Responsive

7. The animation is working in modern browsers, but we can add a **-webkit** vendor prefixed version to support more (older) browsers. Copy the **animation** line of code you just wrote and paste a copy as shown below:

   ```
   .feature-wrap .panorama {
      padding: 10% 0;
      background-image: url(../img/panorama.jpg);
      animation: moving-bg 20s linear infinite alternate;
      animation: moving-bg 20s linear infinite alternate;
   }
   ```

8. Add the **-webkit** vendor prefix to the first one, as shown below in bold:

   ```
   -webkit-animation: moving-bg 20s linear infinite alternate;
   animation: moving-bg 20s linear infinite alternate;
   ```

   NOTE: How long you include a **-webkit** vendor prefixed version of this property will depend on how long you want to support older browsers. For info about browser support refer to caniuse.com/#feat=css-animation

9. The keyframes we made are for the non-vendor prefixed **animation** property. We also need to create keyframes for the **-webkit-animation** property we just added. Scroll to the bottom of **style.css**.

10. Copy the multiple lines of code for the **@keyframes** block of code.

11. Paste the keyframes once below. You should have two identical versions of the following chunk of code:

    ```
    @keyframes moving-bg {
       0% {
          background-position: 0 0;
       }
       100% {
          background-position: 100% 0;
       }
    }
    ```

12. Add the **-webkit** vendor prefix to the first one, as shown below in bold:

    ```
    @-webkit-keyframes moving-bg {
       ( CODE OMITTED TO SAVE SPACE )
    }
    @keyframes moving-bg {
       ( CODE OMITTED TO SAVE SPACE )
    }
    ```

13. Save the file and reload the browser. Take a moment to admire your excellent work! You just created a CSS3 animation from scratch!

1C   Animating the Panorama & Making the Layout Responsive

Disabling the Fixed Background Images on Mobile Devices

In a previous exercise we made the background images remain fixed to the window as we scroll, creating a cool scrolling effect. As we mentioned in that exercise, that scrolling effect won't work on mobile devices, or can cause display issues on iOS. Let's see how we can disable that effect on mobile devices.

1. Return to **style.css** in your code editor.

2. Using CSS media queries we can change the styling of elements based on the size of the web browser. Above the first set of keyframes type the following bold code:

   ```
   @media (max-width: 600px) {

   }
   @-webkit-keyframes moving-bg {
   ```

   NOTE: This code is a **CSS media query**. Any styles placed inside the media query will not be applied, unless the media query is true. This media query means "for any browsers 600 pixels wide or less, use the following styles." A browser wider than 600 pixels would not use the styles we're about to code.

3. Add the following bold code:

   ```
   @media (max-width: 600px) {
       .feature-wrap .photo {
          background-attachment: scroll;
       }
   }
   ```

   NOTE: When two CSS rules target the same element in the same way, they are equally specific. When specificity is equal, a later rule overrides an earlier rule. This rule comes farther down in the code, so it overrides a rule above that sets **background-attachment: fixed;**

4. Save the file and preview it in Chrome (so we can use it's DevTools).

5. Resize the browser window so it's large (more than 600 pixels) and notice that the photo backgrounds are still fixed to the page as you scroll.

6. Resize the browser to be smaller than 600 pixels wide, and notice the backgrounds now scroll along with the page. This will work properly on mobile devices.

7. Resize the window as large as you can make it.

8. To open the DevTools, **Ctrl–click** (Mac) or **Right–click** (Windows) on the page and choose **Inspect**.

Animating the Panorama & Making the Layout Responsive 1C

9. As shown below, at the top left of the DevTools window, click the **Toggle device toolbar** button:

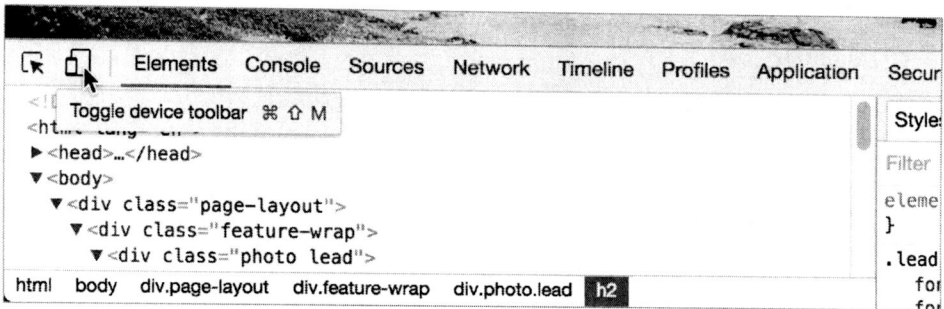

10. As shown below, at the top left of the emulator you can choose a device. As shown below, choose the **iPad Pro**.

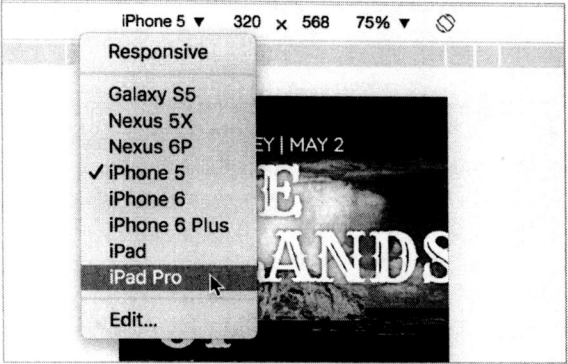

11. Reload the page to make sure it's displayed properly.

12. Scroll the page to see that the background images are fixed. While it appears to work fine in here, Chrome is emulating the iPad Pro size, not the iOS Safari rendering engine. On the iPad these images will be sized wrong and look bad.

    While our CSS media query took care of a large majority of mobile devices, some tablets (such as the iPad) are bigger than the 600px we used and will still have the fixed background attachment (which is a problem on these devices). We could make the media query larger to accommodate them, but the iPad Pro is 1366px when held horizontally. If we make the media that large, we'd disable the scrolling effect for many desktop users that could see it! That's not a good solution.

    CSS can't differentiate between desktop and mobile devices, so we'll need to use a bit of JavaScript. Don't worry if you don't know JavaScript, we've written the code for you!

13. Keep the page open in Chrome with the Device Toolbar open so we can reload it after making some changes.

14. Switch back to your code editor.

15. Open **Hawaii > snippets > mobile-detection.html**

1C   Animating the Panorama & Making the Layout Responsive

16. Select all the code in the file.

17. Copy the code.

18. Close **mobile-detection.html**.

19. Switch to **index.html** in your code editor.

20. Find the **<body>** tag around line line 14.

21. Paste the code just below the **body** tag:

    ```
    <body>
    <script>
       var isMobile = navigator.userAgent.match(/(iPhone|iPod|iPad|Android)/);
       if( isMobile != null ) {
          document.body.className += ' ' + 'mobile';
       }
    </script>
    ```

    This code detects iPhone, iPod, iPad, or Android devices. If it detects one of those mobile devices, it adds a **mobile** class to the **body** tag that we can use to create styles specific to mobile devices.

    Detailed Explanation: When you visit a website, a line of text (called a user agent string) is reported to the browser. Our JavaScript searches that text for iPhone, iPod, iPad, or Android. If it finds one, it returns what it finds, otherwise nothing (null) is returned. If it finds one of those devices, we add a **mobile** class to the **body** tag. We can then use CSS to target mobile devices with the **mobile** class added by JavaScript!

22. Save the file.

23. Return to **style.css**.

24. Find the **.feature-wrap .photo** rule (which starts around line 88) and below that add the following bold code:

    ```
    .feature-wrap .photo {
       background-repeat: no-repeat;
       background-position: center;
       background-size: cover;
       background-attachment: fixed;
    }
    .mobile .feature-wrap .photo {
       background-attachment: scroll;
    }
    ```

    NOTE: This rule will only be applied if JavaScript detects an iPhone, iPod, iPad, or Android device. If someone has JavaScript disabled, the other CSS rule we created in the 600px media query will still take care a lot of mobile devices.

Animating the Panorama & Making the Layout Responsive

25. Switch back to Chrome and reload the page.

    NOTE: While Chrome does not use the iOS Safari rendering engine, this emulator does spoof the user agent string so the page will think that it's on an actual iPad Pro (which means our JavaScript should work).

26. Try scrolling now, and you should see the background images scroll with the page, so it will now work properly in mobile phone and tablets.

27. Close the DevTools window by clicking the X at the top right.

28. Reload the page to make sure it's displayed properly.

29. Try scrolling again, and if the window is more than 600px wide the background images should be fixed. Now the fixed scrolling effect works everywhere we want it to, and is turned off anywhere it won't work. Awesome!

Creating Responsive Layouts with CSS Media Queries

The page is looking pretty good, but when the browser window is small, the text is a bit too large. If someone viewed the site on a mobile browser, the headlines might cover too much of the photos. Let's improve the text sizes based on browser size.

1. Return to **style.css** in your code editor.

2. **Above** the **(max-width: 600px)** media query add the following new media query shown in bold:

   ```
   @media (max-width: 1024px) {


   }
   @media (max-width: 600px) {
   ```

3. Add the following bold code to make the photo highlight text resize in small browser windows:

   ```
   @media (max-width: 1024px) {
       .feature-wrap .text {
           font-size: 2em;
       }
   }
   ```

4. Save the file and reload the browser. Scroll down to the panorama or photo stack. View the browser at a small size and then at a size larger than 1024 pixels wide, noticing the responsive changes in text styles.

5. While the browser is still narrower than 1024 pixels, take note of the panorama animation you created earlier. It's now scaled down to a smaller size and doesn't have very far to pan in either direction. Let's make the panorama larger at this size.

1C Animating the Panorama & Making the Layout Responsive

6. Return to **style.css** in your code editor and at the bottom of the media query, add the following bold code:

   ```
   @media (max-width: 1024px) {
      .feature-wrap .text {
         font-size: 2em;
      }
      .feature-wrap .panorama {
         padding: 15% 0;
      }
   }
   ```

7. Save the file and reload the browser to see the improved panorama at this size. The zooming YouTube video doesn't look as great on small browsers, particularly in the "pre-zoom" state when the video is only 40% of the browser's width. Let's remove the zooming video from small browsers.

8. Switch back to **style.css** in your code editor.

9. Add the following bold code to remove the zooming feature from browsers smaller than 1024 pixels wide:

   ```
   .feature-wrap .panorama {
      padding: 15% 0;
   }
   .zoom {
      width: 100%;
   }
   ```

10. Save the file and reload the browser. Make the browser window smaller than 1024 pixels wide and notice that the zoom feature disappears. However, the space around the video needs to be fixed. Also, when you hover over the video, the space around it changes. Let's fix both of these issues.

11. Return to **style.css** in your code editor.

12. Add the following margins to the **.zoom** rule you just added:

    ```
    .zoom {
       width: 100%;
       margin: 0 0 25px 0;
    }
    ```

13. This should also apply when we **hover** over **.zoom** so add the following bold code. Don't miss the **comma** after the first **.zoom**!

    ```
    .zoom, .zoom:hover {
       width: 100%;
       margin: 0 0 25px 0;
    }
    ```

Animating the Panorama & Making the Layout Responsive

14. Save the file and reload the browser. Make sure your browser window is narrower than 1024 pixels wide, then try hovering over the YouTube video to make sure the problem is fixed. Looking good!

15. Let's create more break points with more alternate styles for smaller browsers. Return to **style.css** in your code editor.

16. Add a new media query before **@media (max-width: 600px)** with the following bold code:

    ```
    @media (max-width: 850px) {

    }
    @media (max-width: 600px) {
    ```

    NOTE: We make all pages work on mobile devices, but some of the effects are targeted only to desktops. While we could have used a mobile first approach to build this page, we thought it more appropriate to use a desktop first approach because desktop users get most of the effects. In the end it will work on all devices, but the desktop first approach means the media queries will use **max** instead of **min**-width and start with large widths and progressively get smaller as you read down the code.

17. This media query will apply only to browsers less than 850 pixels wide. Let's modify the text size and margins at this break point. Add the following bold code:

    ```
    @media (max-width: 850px) {
       .feature-wrap .text {
          font-size: 1.5em;
          margin: 0 5%;
       }
    }
    ```

18. Save the file and reload the browser. Make the browser narrower than 850 pixels and notice the subtly smaller text sizes and margins.

    While in the browser at this size, take a look at the panorama photo again. Earlier, in the 1024 pixel media query, we specified that the panorama should have more padding to make the image larger. Let's further increase the padding of the panorama now that we are at 850 pixels or less.

19. Return to **style.css** in your code editor and add the following bold code:

    ```
    @media (max-width: 850px) {
       .feature-wrap .text {
          font-size: 1.5em;
          margin: 0 5%;
       }
       .feature-wrap .panorama {
          padding: 20% 0;
       }
    }
    ```

1C Animating the Panorama & Making the Layout Responsive

20. The behavior of the photo stack at this size could use refinement. Add the following bold code to the 850 pixel media query, which will refine margins and center the text in the photo stack:

    ```
    .feature-wrap .panorama {
        padding: 20% 0;
    }
    .feature-wrap .stack .text {
        width: auto;
        margin: 0 5%;
        font-size: 3.5em;
        text-align: center;
    }
    ```

21. Save the file and reload the browser. Make the browser narrower than 850 pixels—but wait! The text in the photo stack has strange margins, and it's not centered like we wanted. The problem is specificity: we did not match all the exact class names that we defined earlier.

22. Return to editing **style.css** in your code editor.

23. Fix the issue by adding the following bold code, paying special attention to the **commas** at the end of the first two lines:

    ```
    .feature-wrap .stack .text,
    .feature-wrap .stack .text.right,
    .feature-wrap .stack .text.left {
        width: auto;
        margin: 0 5%;
        font-size: 3.5em;
        text-align: center;
    }
    ```

24. Save the file and reload the browser, resizing the browser window to be narrower than 850 pixels. Take a moment to admire the new centered text on the photo stack!

25. Return to **style.css** in your code editor.

Animating the Panorama & Making the Layout Responsive — 1C

26. At 600 pixels we want the font size to decrease again, and the callout text, rather than being an absurdly narrow column, will occupy the full width of the browser. We already have a media query for 600px, so we can add our styles to it. Add the following bold code to fix the behavior of the **callout** class:

    ```css
    @media (max-width: 600px) {
       .feature-wrap .photo {
          background-attachment: scroll;
       }
       .callout {
          float: none;
          margin: 0;
          width: auto;
       }
    }
    ```

27. Save the file and reload the browser. Try making the window narrower and wider than 600 pixels and see how the **callout** column (near the top of the page) changes responsively!

28. Return to **style.css** in your code editor.

29. Let's create one more rule to make the photo stack text even smaller for browsers under 600 pixels. Add the following bold code:

    ```css
    .callout {
       float: none;
       margin: 0;
       width: auto;
    }
    .feature-wrap .stack .text,
    .feature-wrap .stack .text.right,
    .feature-wrap .stack .text.left {
       font-size: 2.5em;
    }
    }
    ```

30. Save the file and reload the browser. Notice the way the photo stack text changes responsively when you resize the browser window!

    The webpage is complete but if you would like to continue to use media queries to add even more refinement to the web-font typography at different break points, continue on!

Optional Bonus: More Media Query Refinements

We can fine-tune typography to our heart's content by using **media queries,** and here are a few more ways we could refine the page.

1C Animating the Panorama & Making the Layout Responsive

1. Return to editing **style.css** in your code editor.

2. Add the following bold code to the **1024px** media query:

   ```
   @media (max-width: 1024px) {
      .lead h1 {
         font-size: 3.2em;
      }
      .lead h2 {
         font-size: 1.45em;
      }
      .lead h3 {
         font-size: 0.95em;
      }
      .feature-wrap .text {
   ```

3. Save the file and reload the browser. Try resizing the browser window slowly, from a very large window to a very small window, and keep an eye on the way the feature head behaves responsively. No matter the browser size, every viewer will have a customized appearance!

4. Return to **style.css** in your code editor.

5. Copy the styles for **.lead h1**, **.lead h2** and **.lead h3** that you just typed.

6. Paste them in the 850 pixel media query as follows:

   ```
   @media (max-width: 850px) {
      .lead h1 {
         font-size: 3.2em;
      }
      .lead h2 {
         font-size: 1.45em;
      }
      .lead h3 {
         font-size: 0.95em;
      }
      .feature-wrap .text {
   ```

7. Change the values as follows:

   ```
   @media (max-width: 850px) {
      .lead h1 {
         font-size: 2.4em;
      }
      .lead h2 {
         font-size: 1.05em;
      }
      .lead h3 {
         font-size: 0.75em;
      }
   ```

Animating the Panorama & Making the Layout Responsive 1C

8. Save the file and preview **index.html** in a WebKit browser (either Safari or Chrome) if you aren't already.

   Resize the browser window. Notice the headings over the lead (first photo) should look better across the various sizes.

Webkit Font Smoothing

We have one final typographic refinement to take care of. Take a quick look at the heading that says **THE ISLANDS OF HAWAII**. Don't the letters look a bit fat, especially around the "cut-outs" in the typeface? WebKit browsers automatically make web fonts a bit "chubbier," so to make the Rye font on our site look a bit truer to the original, we can change the anti-alias settings.

1. Return to **style.css** in your code editor.

2. Find the **.lead h1** rule around line 32 and add the following bold code:

   ```
   .lead h1 {
      font-family: 'Rye', cursive;
      font-weight: 400;
      font-size: 3.6em;
      line-height: 1em;
      text-transform: uppercase;
      margin: 1% 10% 0 10%;
      -webkit-font-smoothing: antialiased;
   }
   ```

3. Copy the line of code you just wrote.

4. Find the other place we used the Rye font, in the **.feature-wrap .text** rule starting around line 119, and paste the code as follows:

   ```
   .feature-wrap .text {
      font-family: 'Rye', sans-serif;
      font-size: 3em;
      line-height: 1.1em;
      color: #f1f1f1;
      text-align: center;
      margin: 0 25%;
      text-shadow: 0 0 4px rgba(0,0,0, 0.5);
      -webkit-font-smoothing: antialiased;
   }
   ```

1C Animating the Panorama & Making the Layout Responsive

5. Save the file and reload **index.html** in a WebKit browser such as Chrome or Safari. Take note of what the "cutouts" in the Rye font look like before and after the reload. They should be more noticeable and truer to the original font.

   The webpage is now complete, with refined web-font typography and a plethora of exciting CSS3 features!

   NOTE: There is some debate as to whether the **-webkit-font-smoothing** setting should be used. It does not affect all browsers so the type will render differently in Firefox, for example. But type renders differently on Mac vs. Windows, so that's part of the nature of the web. It's good to know about, but it's up to you to decide whether or not you want to use it.

Check Out
OUR OTHER WORKBOOKS!

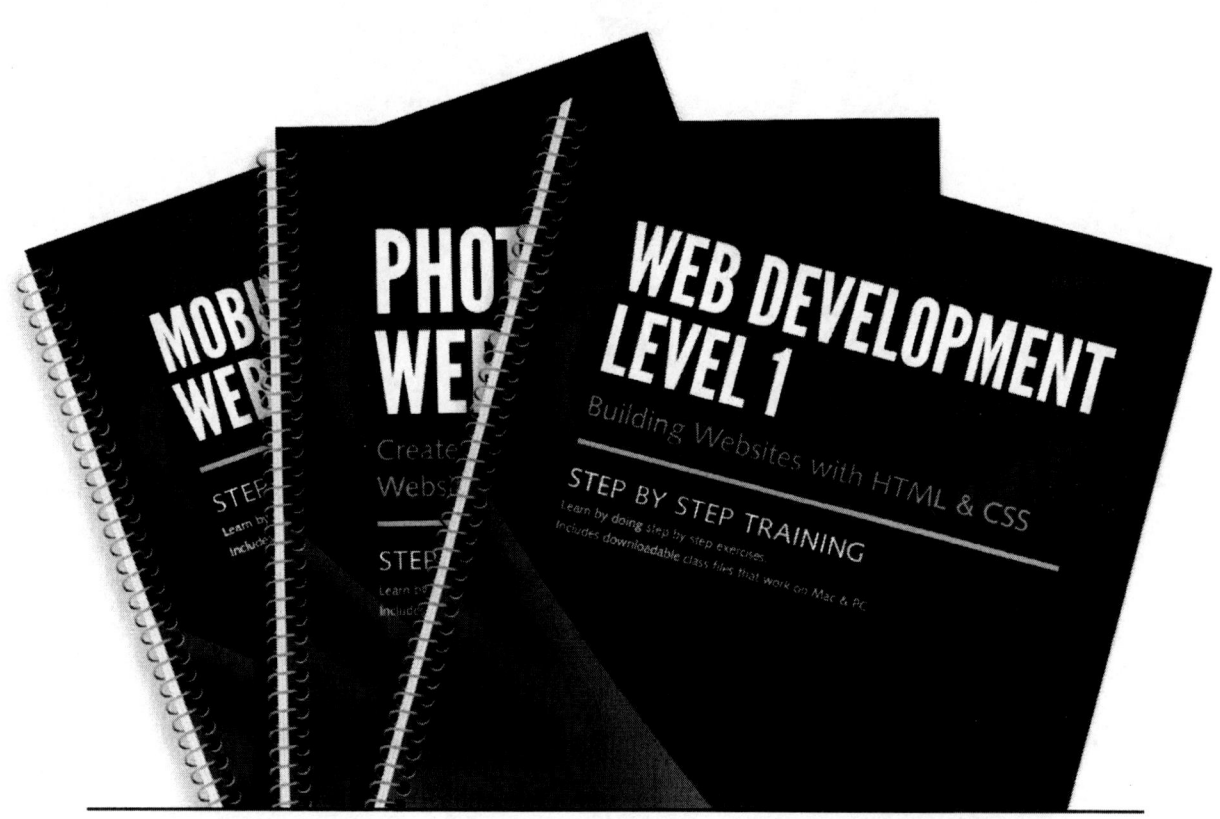

Web Development Level 1 and 2

JavaScript & jQuery

GreenSock Animation

Mobile & Responsive Web Design

WordPress

PHP & MySQL

Ruby on Rails

Photoshop for Web & UI

Photoshop Animated GIFs

Adobe Experience Design

Sketch

HTML Email

Responsive HTML Email

PowerPoint

Adobe InDesign

Adobe Illustrator

Adobe Photoshop

Photoshop Advanced

Adobe Lightroom

Adobe After Effects

Adobe CC: Intro to InDesign, Photoshop, & Illustrator

NOBLEDESKTOP.COM/BOOKS